Serve It Up!

A Friendship Cookbook

ISBN 0-439-22348-2

Illustrations by Maj Hagsted
Design by Julie Mullarkey

12 11 10 9 8 7 6 5 4 3   5 6/0
Printed in China
First Scholastic printing, July 2001

Serve It Up!

A Friendship Cookbook

by Lia Haberman

Scholastic Inc.
New York Toronto London Auckland Sydney Mexico City
New Delhi Hong Kong

Table of Contents

Intro

Food and friendship are closely tied together. You spend lunch with your class chums, share an after-school snack with your best buds, and invite your favorite friends over for a weekend supper. Shouldn't the food you chow down reflect the quality of your friendship? So instead of eating store-bought snacks or ordering a pizza to go, why not get into the kitchen

and whip something up? Even better, invite your friends: Cooking together is a lot of fun! While one of you is chopping, the other can stir or sizzle. (Plus cleaning up—yawn—is a lot easier when you've got company.)

To make sure you're set, every chapter in this book covers something new, whether you're looking for a veggie lunch, fast snacks you can whip up after school, slumber-party finger foods and a morning-after breakfast, or lots of gooey desserts everyone will want to share.

The techniques in this book are so simple that even if you've never cooked before, you can do them! With every recipe, there's a list of kitchen appliances and ingredients you'll need so you'll know before starting if you've got everything. And there are lots of practical tips to make sure you get the best results.

So what are you waiting for? Gather your BFF or a bunch of your friends in the kitchen and get cooking. The good vibes practically guarantee a great meal—plus, you're sure to have a lot of fun together!

Handy Hints

Always read a recipe all the way through first to make sure you've got the ingredients and kitchen appliances you need. Nothing's more annoying than getting halfway through a recipe and realizing you don't have a key ingredient.

Get all your ingredients and kitchen appliances together before you start working so you've got easy access to everything you need.

Wash your hands before you begin and be sure that all the utensils you plan to use have been washed, too.

Be sure to ask your folks for permission before cooking anything on the stove or in the oven. They may want to be around to help out.

Before you start a recipe that calls for baking something, preheat the oven to the right temperature. If you put your cakes or cookies in the oven when it's still cold, they won't cook properly.

Try to measure ingredients as carefully as possible. Too much or too little of something, even chocolate, could make your food taste terrible.

Always use solid butter or margarine (the kind that comes in a stick) when baking cakes or cookies; the cookies or cakes that you make with the spreadable stuff won't hold their shape.

If a recipe calls for butter or margarine at room temperature, take it out of the fridge at least a half hour before you start cooking. If you absolutely have no time to spare, wash your hands well, then mash the butter or margarine with your fingers. Your body heat will bring it to room temperature.

When handling sharp knives, hold them by the handle with the blade pointed away from you.

Most of the recipes in this book are for four people, unless they're marked otherwise. To double a recipe, just use twice the amount of each ingredient; to halve a recipe, cut the ingredients by half.

When inviting your friends over for a home-cooked meal or even just a snack, make sure you know their particular tastes. If one of your friends is a vegetarian, she won't really dig the deli slice sandwiches, or if she's allergic to something like nuts, you don't want to include them in your brownies.

Chapter One:
The Breakfast Club

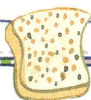

Let's say you're having a sleepover. You've got every detail planned, from the movie rental full of hotties and the bowl of buttery popcorn to the late-night ghost stories and rounds of Truth or Dare. But what are you going to feed your friends in the morning? Have no fear! Here's some tasty breakfast chow for morning-after sleepover success. All the recipes—from sparkling glasses of orangeade to cinnamon-flavored French toast—are easy to make, so you won't have to get up early (that is: ahead of your friends) when you want to sleep late!

Orangeade

This juice and seltzer combo gives your morning OJ a kick!

Ingredients You'll Need:

6 cups fresh orange juice
4½ cups chilled seltzer or club soda
ice

Utensils You'll Need:

pitcher or jug
4 glasses

What You Do:

Mix everything in the pitcher and stir.
Pour into the glasses and enjoy!

Fruity Granola Yogurt Parfait

(serves four)

This morning treat looks really super and tastes really great—the bonus is it only takes about five minutes to make.

Ingredients You'll Need:

2 cups granola
2 eight-ounce cartons vanilla yogurt
2 cups fruit chunks, like melon, pineapple, strawberries, blueberries, or bananas

Utensils You'll Need:

4 sundae glasses (or just 4 tall glasses)
spoon

What You Do:

Place a couple of spoonfuls of yogurt in the bottom of each glass, then sprinkle with a layer of granola and a layer of fruit. Repeat each layer until you've used up all your ingredients.

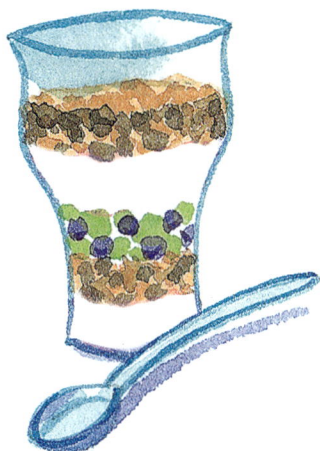

French Toast Fingers

(serves four to eight)

French toast is yummy and so easy to make.

Ingredients You'll Need:

3 eggs
1 cup milk
½ teaspoon cinnamon
8 slices bread
2 tablespoons butter or margarine
Maple syrup

Utensils You'll Need:

Knife   Frying pan
Whisk   Spatula
Mixing bowl

What You Do:

Cut each piece of bread into four slices or fingers. (Cutting your French toast into fingers helps the bread cook more evenly than using a whole slice—plus, it just looks cooler!) Beat together the eggs, milk, and cinnamon. Melt half of the butter in a frying pan over medium heat. Dip each bread finger into the egg mixture so it's totally coated. Place them in the frying pan and cook for about two minutes on each side or until they're golden brown. You'll probably be able to fit about four fingers in a medium-sized skillet and around six to eight in a large skillet. Add the rest of the butter to the frying pan if the pan starts to get sticky. Dish up with lots of maple syrup.

Cinnamon Toast

(serves four to eight)

Another quick and great breakfast recipe. It also makes a great after-school snack.

Ingredients You'll Need:

8 slices bread
2 tablespoons butter or margarine
8 teaspoons sugar
4 teaspoons cinnamon

Utensils You'll Need:

Mixing bowl
Toaster
Measuring spoons
Butter knife

What You Do:

Mix the sugar and cinnamon in a bowl. Toast the bread and, while it's still hot, spread each piece with about ¼ tablespoon of butter. Sprinkle a little more than a teaspoon of cinnamon sugar on each piece of toast.

My Own Breakfast Recipes

Chapter Two:
The Lunch Bunch

The next time your friends come over for lunch, get creative together in the kitchen by putting a new spin on some of your old favorites. It's just as easy, let's say, to make a Peanut-butter-and-banana or peanut-butter-and-Marshmallow-Fluff sandwich as it is to make a peanut-butter-and-jelly sandwich. Likewise, don't just settle for a plain ol' grilled cheese when you can stuff your sandwich with extra fixings like avocados and tomatoes.

Maybe you've just come from soccer practice or a swim meet and need something warm and filling, or you may not be feeling very hungry and just want to graze on a crunchy salad. Whatever you're craving, you'll find some tasty treats in this chapter!

Not Your Mom's PB&J

Forget plain old PB&J! There's a restaurant in New York City where they make peanut butter sandwiches with a zillion different combos—and so can you.

Ingredients You'll Need:

8 slices bread
1 jar peanut butter
1 banana
2 tablespoons honey
2 tablespoons Marshmallow Fluff
2 tablespoons applesauce

Utensils You'll Need:

Butter knife
Measuring spoon

What You Do:

Spread a little peanut butter on four pieces of bread and top each slice with a different topping— banana, honey, Marshmallow Fluff, or applesauce. Close your sandwiches, cut off the crusts, and cut them each into four quarters so you and your friends get a taste of each sandwich.

Sizzling Mini Sandwiches

These hot packets fresh out of the oven are hard to resist and make for a totally satisfying sandwich.

Ingredients You'll Need:

4 English muffins
8 cheese slices
8 deli slices of turkey, ham, or bologna
4 teaspoons mayo
4 teaspoons mustard

Utensils You'll Need:

Measuring spoon
Butter knife
Aluminum foil

What You Do:

Preheat the oven to 375° F. Split your muffins in half. Spread a spoonful of mayo and mustard on the four top halves of the English muffins. Place two slices of cheese and two deli slices each on the four bottom halves. Close the sandwiches and wrap each one in aluminum foil. Place the sandwiches in the oven and bake for 10 to 15 minutes or until the cheese has melted. Yum!

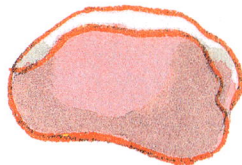

The Best Grilled Cheese Ever

Here's a cheesy sandwich that's a super update on your basic grilled cheese.

Ingredients You'll Need:

8 slices bread
8 slices American, cheddar,
  or other cheese—whatever
  kinds you like!
8 slices avocado
4 slices tomato
2 tablespoons butter

Utensils You'll Need:

Frying pan
Butter knife

What You Do:

Butter one side of each slice of bread. On the unbuttered side, place two pieces of cheese, two pieces of avocado, and one slice of tomato. Close the sandwich and butter the top. Place the sandwiches in the frying pan, and set the pan on the stove. Cook at medium heat until golden brown, about three minutes, then flip and cook the other side for about three minutes. You might be able to do only two sandwiches at a time unless you've got a giant pan to cook in.

Do-it-yourself Veggie Wraps

Set up everything before your friends arrive so they can each make their own wrap—kind of like an ice-cream sundae bar, only all your toppings are veggies!

Ingredients You'll Need:

4 wraps (or tortilla shells)
4 ounces spreadable cream cheese
2 tomatoes, chopped
1 small cucumber, sliced
1 avocado, sliced
2 shredded carrots
sprouts
lettuce, shredded
2 large mushrooms, sliced (optional)
½ onion (optional)
4 broccoli florets, sliced into
    small pieces (optional)

Utensils You'll Need:

Cutting knife
Butter knife
Condiment bowls

What You Do:

Put all the veggies in bowls and arrange on a table for easy selection. Smear the inside of the wraps with cream cheese. Then let your friends add veggies to make their wraps. Yum!

Broccoli-Cauliflower Salad

The dressing turns the broccoli and cauliflower softer on the outside but still crunchy on the inside.

Ingredients You'll Need:

2½ cups broccoli florets
2½ cups cauliflower florets
1 small red pepper, finely chopped
1 small onion, finely chopped
¾ cup of your favorite salad dressing, like Italian,
    Russian, ranch, or blue cheese

Utensils You'll Need:

Mixing bowl
Measuring cup
Cutting knife

What You Do:

Toss all the salad ingredients together with the salad dressing in the mixing bowl, and then refrigerate till you're ready to serve.

My Own Lunchtime Recipes

Chapter Three:
After-school Snack Attack

Here are a bunch of tasty recipes to try with your friends, from a hot cheese dip you can serve with nachos to some spicy popcorn. The best part is that these recipes take almost no time to make (especially when you've got friends helping).

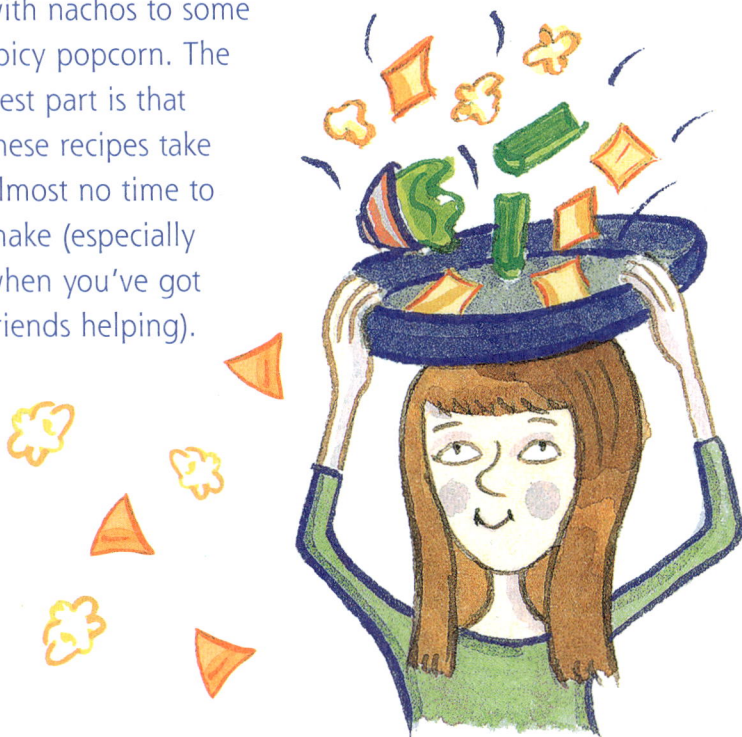

Ants on a Log

The traditional recipe for Ants on a Log calls for peanut butter, but for a tasty change you could also fill your celery stalks with spreadable cheese or garden vegetable cream cheese.

Ingredients You'll Need:

4 celery stalks
8 tablespoons peanut butter
¼ cup raisins

Utensils You'll Need:

Measuring cup and spoons
Butter knife

What You Do:

Wash and dry the celery. Cut the celery stalks in half so you now have eight pieces. Spread a tablespoon of peanut butter into each piece of celery and dot with raisins.

Spicy Popcorn

Whether you make popcorn in the microwave, on the stovetop, or in a popcorn maker, spice it up with one of these suggested toppings.

Ingredients You'll Need:
Popcorn

Top with one of the following:
1 teaspoon Tabasco sauce
¼ cup grated Parmesan cheese
1 tablespoon balsamic vinegar

Utensils You'll Need:
Mixing bowl

What You Do:
Make the popcorn as you normally would, and put it in the bowl. Add one of the suggested toppings, a little at a time for a totally new taste!

Hot Cheese Dip

You and your friends won't be able to get enough of this yummy dip!

Ingredients You'll Need:
1 cup (sliced and cubed) Velveeta cheese
½ cup chunky salsa
Non-stick cooking spray
1 bag tortilla chips

Utensils You'll Need:
Small saucepan
Measuring cup
Wooden spoon
Serving bowl

What You Do:
Lightly coat your saucepan with non-stick cooking spray. Over low heat, melt the Velveeta in the saucepan, stirring constantly so the cheese doesn't stick to the bottom. When the cheese is melted completely, take it off the stove, stir the salsa into the melted cheese, pour into a bowl, and serve with tortilla chips.

Veggies and Dip

You can use any vegetables for this snack classic. Just make sure to cut them up into bite-size pieces.

Ingredients You'll Need:

1 cup mayo
1 cup sour cream
1 package onion soup mix
1 bag baby carrots
2 red peppers, sliced into strips
1 head of raw broccoli or cauliflower florets

Utensils You'll Need:

Mixing bowl
Serving platter
Cutting knife
Spoon

What You Do:

To make the dip, stir the mayo, sour cream, and onion soup mix together. Allow the dip to sit for fifteen minutes so that the ingredients blend together and the onion soup mix softens. Arrange the vegetables on a platter and serve to your friends with the dip.

Stuffed Caps

If you're a fan of mushrooms, try this cheesy recipe! It's a great combo of mushroom caps stuffed with cream cheese with lots of herbs and garlic in it.

Ingredients You'll Need:

8 medium to large mushrooms
8 tablespoons herb and/or
   garlic cream cheese
Non-stick cooking spray

Utensils You'll Need:

Baking sheet
Measuring spoon

What You Do:

Preheat the oven to 375° F. Gently wipe the mushrooms clean with a damp cloth and remove the stems (they pull out easily). Place a spoonful of cheese in the hollow where the stems used to be. Arrange the mushrooms cheese side up on a baking sheet and bake for 10 to 15 minutes or until the cheese is lightly browned on top.

My Own Snack Recipes

....

....

....

....

....

....

....

....

....

....

....

....

....

....

....

....

....

....

Chapter Four: Cookie Craze

Wouldn't it be fun to have a party where everyone bakes a batch of their favorite cookies to bring with them? Then at the party everyone would trade their cookies so that they'd have a bunch of different kinds to enjoy. But no, you and your friends don't have to make every single cookie recipe in this chapter all at once—that would be hundreds of cookies! But you *could* try one new recipe each time you get together. (Then again, hundreds of cookies would be kind of fun, wouldn't it?)

Handy Hint:

If you like your cookies soft and chewy, after you take them out of the oven, let them cool for a few minutes, then cover 'em up in a cookie tin or jar. If you prefer your cookies crispy, store them in a tin but don't put the cover on.

Chocolate Chip Cookies

(makes about 72 cookies)

This recipe is supposed to make about six dozen cookies, but somehow you never end up with that many. Could it be because everyone likes to eat the yummy dough before it ever makes it into the oven?

Ingredients You'll Need:

2 sticks butter or margarine, at room temperature
¾ cup sugar
¾ cup packed light brown sugar
2 teaspoons vanilla
2 eggs
2¼ cups unsifted all-purpose flour
1 teaspoon baking soda
½ teaspoon salt
2 cups chocolate chips

Utensils You'll Need:

Electric or hand mixer
2 mixing bowls
Measuring cups and spoons
Cookie sheet

What You Do:

Preheat the oven to 375° F. Beat the butter or margarine, white and brown sugar, and vanilla in a large mixing bowl until light and fluffy. Add the eggs and continue to beat. These are your "wet" ingredients. In a separate bowl, measure out the flour, baking soda, and salt. Mix these dry ingredients together. Gradually add the dry mixture to the wet mixture. Add the chocolate chips and continue to stir until well mixed. Drop by teaspoonfuls onto the ungreased cookie sheet. Bake for eight to ten minutes or until lightly browned.

Peanut Butter Cookies

(makes about 72 cookies)

Make these peanut butter cookies plain and they're delicious. But to make them super-special, just add two cups of chocolate chips.

Ingredients You'll Need:

2 eggs
1 cup peanut butter
1½ sticks butter or margarine,
  at room temperature
½ cup sugar
1 cup packed light brown sugar
2 cups all-purpose flour
2 teaspoons baking soda
¼ teaspoon salt
½ teaspoon cinnamon

Utensils You'll Need:

Electric or hand mixer
2 mixing bowls
Measuring cups and spoons
Cookie sheet
Fork

What You Do:

Preheat the oven to 375° F. Beat the eggs, peanut butter, butter, sugar, and brown sugar in one of the mixing bowls until light and fluffy. This is your "wet" mixture. Measure out the flour, baking soda, salt, and cinnamon into the other bowl and mix together. Gradually beat into the wet mixture. Stir until well mixed. Drop by teaspoonfuls onto the ungreased cookie sheet and flatten each cookie with a fork. (If the fork gets sticky, dip it into a glass of warm water.) Bake for 12 to 15 minutes or until golden brown.

Oatmeal Raisin Cookies

(makes about 40 cookies)

It's oatmeal, it's raisins—it's practically healthy!

Ingredients You'll Need:

1½ sticks butter or margarine,
  at room temperature
¾ cup brown sugar
½ cup sugar
1 egg
2 tablespoons water
2 teaspoons vanilla
¾ cup all-purpose flour
¾ teaspoon baking soda
2 cups instant oatmeal
1½ cups raisins

Utensils You'll Need:

Electric or hand mixer   Measuring cups   Measuring spoons
2 mixing bowls   Cookie sheet

What You Do:

Preheat the oven to 350° F. Beat the first six ingredients together in a mixing bowl until the mixture is light and fluffy. Stir the flour, baking soda, and oatmeal together in a separate bowl. Gradually add the dry ingredients to the wet mixture and beat until all the ingredients are well mixed. Stir in the raisins. Drop by teaspoonfuls onto an ungreased cookie sheet and bake for 12 to 15 minutes or until golden brown.

Snickerdoodles

(makes about 60 cookies)

Funny name, but the cookies taste great!

Ingredients You'll Need:

2 sticks butter or margarine, at room temperature

1½ cups sugar

2 eggs

2¾ cups all-purpose flour

2 teaspoons cream of tartar

1 teaspoon baking soda

½ teaspoon salt

2 tablespoons sugar

2 teaspoons cinnamon

Utensils You'll Need:

3 mixing bowls

Electric or hand mixer

Measuring cups and spoons

Baking sheet

What You Do:

Beat the butter, sugar, and eggs together in a mixing bowl. In a separate bowl, mix together the flour, cream of tartar, baking soda, and salt, and then stir into the wet mixture till the batter is well mixed. Chill the dough in the fridge for about two hours. Preheat the oven to 400° F. Mix the sugar and cinnamon together in a small bowl.

Roll the cold dough into small balls, about a teaspoon each. Roll each ball in the sugar and cinnamon mixture. Place the balls on a cookie sheet and bake for eight to ten minutes.

My Own Cookie Recipes

Chapter Five:
Slumber Party Soiree

Since this is for a slumber party, a bunch of finger foods are fun to make, like Pigs in Blankets (which are hot dogs wrapped up in pastry) and a spinach dip. Special cocktail drinks are fun, too, like Shirley Temples, which you can enjoy while messing around in the kitchen. And for dessert? Just the right mix of fruit and gooey chocolate!

Pigs in Blankets

This is one of the easiest snacks to make and is soooo good. And if any of your friends is a vegetarian, or just for variety, you can replace some of the hot dogs with veggie or tofu dogs.

Ingredients You'll Need:

8 hot dogs or veggie dogs
1 package (8) Pillsbury Crescent Rolls
½ stick butter
¼ cup mustard

Utensils You'll Need:

Measuring cup
Teaspoon
Butter knife
Baking sheet

What You Do:

Preheat the oven to 375° F.
Spread a teaspoon of butter
and a teaspoon of mustard on
each pastry triangle before placing the hot dog on top
and rolling it up. (The hot dog should be sticking out
on both sides.) Bake for ten minutes or until the pastry
is fluffy and golden brown.

Cheesy Chicken Fingers

Serve these up with ketchup, barbecue sauce, or your favorite dressing.

Ingredients You'll Need:

1 package (about 12) uncooked chicken tenders
1 egg, beaten
¾ cup bread crumbs
¼ cup grated Parmesan cheese
1 pinch salt
1 pinch black pepper
Non-stick cooking spray

Utensils You'll Need:

2 mixing bowls
Whisk
Baking sheet

What You Do:

Preheat the oven to 375° F. Lightly coat the baking sheet with non-stick cooking spray. Beat the egg in one bowl. Mix the bread crumbs, Parmesan cheese, salt, and pepper in the other bowl. Dip the chicken tenders into the beaten egg, then toss them around in the bread crumb mixture. Place the chicken tenders on the baking sheet. Spray the chicken lightly with the non-stick cooking spray and bake for 15 minutes. To check if they're done, cut one open to see if the chicken is white. If it's still pink, it's not cooked yet.

Potato Wedges

Baking these potato wedges with a bit of olive oil turns the skin crisp and golden while the inside stays nice and soft.

Ingredients You'll Need:

2 pounds russet potatoes
1 tablespoon olive oil
1 teaspoon salt
Ketchup
Garlic mayo (see recipe, next page)

Utensils You'll Need:

Mixing bowl
Vegetable knife
Cutting board
Baking sheet
Measuring spoons

What You Do:

Preheat oven to 450° F. Wash the potatoes. Slice them in half lengthwise and then cut them lengthwise again into wedges. Toss them in a bowl with the oil and salt, then spread them onto a baking sheet, and place them in the oven. Roast for 30 minutes or until the skins are a nice crispy golden brown. Serve the potatoes with ketchup or garlic mayo.

Garlic Mayo

This dip is so easy to make and tastes so good.

Ingredients You'll Need:

4 tablespoons mayo
1 teaspoon store-bought ready-made crushed garlic
1 teaspoon lemon juice

Utensils You'll Need:

Measuring spoons
Mixing bowl
Whisk

What You Do:

Mix all the ingredients in the
bowl and serve with potato
wedges. Yum!

Spinach Dip

Even if you think you don't like spinach, it's hard not to like this dip.

Ingredients You'll Need:

2 cups sour cream

1 teaspoon store-bought ready-made crushed garlic

1 package (10 ounces) frozen spinach, thawed and drained

2 tablespoons Worcestershire sauce

2 dashes Tabasco sauce

½ teaspoon salt

Big round sourdough loaf
   (or any other round bread)

Utensils You'll Need:

Mixing bowl

Measuring cup and spoons

Bread knife

What You Do:

In a mixing bowl, combine all the ingredients except the bread. Stir together till all the ingredients are well mixed, and then chill in the fridge for about two hours. Slice about a half inch off the top of the bread. Without breaking the crust, carefully pull out all the bread in chunks so you've got a deep bread-crust bowl. (You're going to dip the bread chunks into the dip.) Spoon the dip into the bread-crust bowl and serve with the bread chunks on the side.

Pecan Squares

This gooey mixture of pecans, chocolate chips, and coconut probably seems good enough to eat raw but wait till you taste it warm. Delicious!

Ingredients You'll Need:

Non-stick cooking spray
1⅓ cups Oreo cookie crumbs
  (or chocolate graham
  cracker crumbs
⅓ cup melted butter or margarine
½ cup chocolate chips
½ cup sweetened shredded coconut

½ cup white chocolate chips
½ cup pecans
1 small can condensed milk

Utensils You'll Need:

2 mixing bowls
Measuring cups
8-inch square cake pan

What You Do:

Preheat the oven to 350° F. Lightly coat the cake pan with non-stick cooking spray. Mix the melted butter and cookie crumbs till the mixture is sticky and press into the pan, covering just the bottom. Bake for eight minutes till crispy. Meanwhile, mix together the chocolate chips, white chocolate chips, pecans, coconut, and condensed milk. When the cookie crumbs have cooked, spread the gooey mixture on top and return to the oven for 15 to 20 minutes or until the chips have started to melt and the top begins to brown.

Stuffed Banana Boats

This is a Girl Scout camp classic, but you and your friends don't have to be sitting around a campfire to enjoy these tasty treats!

Ingredients You'll Need:

4 bananas
12 marshmallows
½ cup chocolate chips

Utensils You'll Need:

Cutting knife
Measuring cup
Aluminum foil

What You Do:

Preheat the oven to 375° F. Cut a long slit down the front of each banana, leaving the peel on. Squeeze two to three marshmallows and as many chocolate chips as possible into the opening. Wrap each banana in aluminum foil. Bake in the oven for 10 to 15 minutes.

Quick Tip: Be super-careful when you unwrap the banana packages because the melted chocolate chips and marshmallow goo will be steaming hot.

Cocktails

Sometimes plain old soda just isn't going to cut it. Here are some sophisticated drinks to serve to your friends for special sleepover zip.

Shirley Temple

Ingredients You'll Need Per Person:
6 ounces (or a half can) ginger ale
3 ice cubes
½ teaspoon maraschino cherry juice
Maraschino cherry
Lemon slice

Utensils You'll Need:
Measuring spoon
Glass

What You Do:
Pour the ginger ale into your glass over the ice cubes. Stir in the maraschino cherry juice and maraschino cherry. Top with the lemon slice and serve.

Mint Julep

Ingredients You'll Need Per Person:

3 ice cubes, crushed
6 ounces (or a half can) ginger ale
1 teaspoon superfine sugar (superfine dissolves
    better, but you can use regular white sugar)
4 sprigs fresh mint

Utensils You'll Need:

Sealable plastic baggie
Measuring spoon
Glass

What You Do:

Crush the ice by putting
the cubes in the baggie and
whacking the baggie against
the countertop. Empty the
ice bits into the glass and
stir in the ginger ale and
superfine sugar. Decorate
with mint sprigs.

Roy Rogers

Ingredients You'll Need Per Person:

6 ounces (or a half can) ginger ale
2 ounces (or a ¼ cup) lemon-lime soda
3 ice cubes
1 teaspoon maraschino cherry juice
Maraschino cherry
Orange slice

Utensils You'll Need:

Measuring spoon
Glass

What You Do:

Pour the ginger ale and lemon-lime soda into your glass over the ice cubes. Stir in the maraschino cherry juice and add the maraschino cherry. Top with the orange slice.

My Own Party Recipes

Chapter Six:
The Supper Club

There are two menu ideas in this chapter for you and your friends to make supper. One is Italian inspired with Caesar salad, a gooey baked spaghetti casserole, and an easy-to-make chocolate–cherry cake for dessert. The other is a Tex–Mex-themed fiesta that includes nachos, guacamole, and spicy pizza. They both make a great start to a fun sleepover or a girls' night "in."

An Italian Feast

Caesar Salad

Sure, you order Caesar salad when you go out to eat, but it isn't hard to make at home!

Ingredients You'll Need:

1 head romaine lettuce
½ cup croutons
½ cup grated Parmesan cheese
½ cup mayo
½ teaspoon store-bought
   crushed garlic
1 tablespoon lemon juice
1 teaspoon Worcestershire sauce
1 pinch salt
1 pinch black pepper

Utensils You'll Need:

Salad bowl   Measuring cups and spoons
Mixing bowl   Fork

What You Do:

Wash and dry the lettuce. Tear it into small pieces and put it in the salad bowl. In the mixing bowl, whisk together the mayo, crushed garlic, lemon juice, Worcestershire sauce, salt, and pepper with the fork. Toss this mixture with the lettuce, then top the salad with croutons and Parmesan cheese.

Baked Spaghetti

This gooey pasta dish is great. You just toss everything together and bake—what could be easier?

Ingredients You'll Need:

12 ounces uncooked spaghetti (¾ of a package)
2 cups spaghetti sauce
1½ cups Velveeta cheese, cut into chunks
1 pinch salt
1 pinch black pepper

Utensils You'll Need:

Large saucepan
Measuring cups
2-pint (4-cup) casserole dish

What You Do:

Preheat the oven to 375° F. Boil a pot of water and cook the spaghetti according to the directions on the box. Meanwhile, mix the spaghetti sauce, 1 cup of the Velveeta cheese chunks, salt, and pepper in the casserole dish. When done, drain the spaghetti and put it in the casserole dish with the sauce and cheese mixture. Mix together until the ingredients are evenly distributed in the dish. Top with the remaining ½ cup Velveeta cubes. Bake for 20 minutes or until the casserole is golden brown.

Chocolate-Cherry Cake

This is a simpler version of a popular dessert called Black Forest cake. The flavor combo of chocolate, cherries, and whipped cream is amazing! ·

Ingredients You'll Need:

1 package chocolate cake mix
   Note: You may need eggs, water, and cooking oil for the cake mixture. Please read the box well and make sure you have all the ingredients you need before you begin.
3 cups of Cool Whip whipped topping
1 can (21 ounces) of cherry pie filling

Utensils You'll Need:

2 mixing bowls
Measuring cups
2 eight-inch round cake pans

What You Do:

Mix the cake according to the directions on the box. Then follow the baking instructions on the back of the box. In a separate mixing bowl, gently stir together the Cool Whip and cherry pie filling. When the cake has cooled, sandwich the two layers together with cherry cream filling, then use the rest of the cherry cream to cover the top of the cake.

A Tex-Mex Feast

Nachos

Sure, you could just serve tortilla chips and salsa, but the more toppings you pile on, the tastier this dish gets!

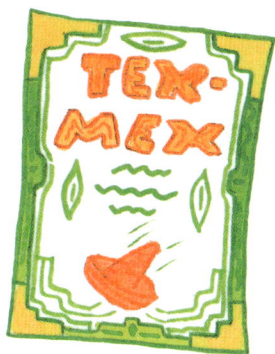

Ingredients You'll Need:
8 ounces nacho chips
½ cup chunky salsa
½ cup shredded cheddar cheese
Guacamole, sour cream, extra salsa (optional)

Utensils You'll Need:
Baking sheet
Measuring cups

What You Do:
Set your oven temperature to broil. Lay the nacho chips out on a baking sheet. Spoon the salsa over the chips and top with the shredded cheese. Place under the broiler for five minutes or until the cheese has melted. Serve with guacamole (see recipe, page 60), sour cream, and more salsa, if desired.

Guacamole

Grab a friend to help make this crowd-pleaser and take turns mashing the avocado into mush.

Ingredients You'll Need:

2 avocados
1 teaspoon crushed garlic
1 tablespoon salsa
1 pinch salt
Bag of tortilla chips

Utensils You'll Need:

Cutting knife
Spoon
Mixing bowl
Fork
Measuring spoons

What You Do:

Slice the avocados in half and pull them apart. Scoop out the flesh and throw away the skin and the seed. Mash the avocado in the mixing bowl with a fork. When well mashed, stir in the garlic, salsa, and salt. Serve with tortilla chips or nachos (see recipe, page 59).

Tex-Mex Pizza

Not quite the standard pie you might be used to, but this spicy version tastes just as good.

Ingredients You'll Need:
1 twelve-inch prebaked pizza crust
1 can (16 ounces) refried beans
1 cup chunky salsa
1 cup shredded Monterey Jack or cheddar cheese

Utensils You'll Need:
Baking sheet
Measuring cups
Pizza cutter

What You Do:
Preheat the oven to 450° F. Spread the refried beans evenly over the pizza crust. Top with salsa, then the shredded cheese. Place on the baking sheet and bake for 15 minutes or until the cheese is melted.

Fruit Kabobs

This is such an easy dessert, and it looks really colorful and exotic.

Ingredients You'll Need:

4 cups fruit chunks, like melon, pineapple, strawberries, kiwi, and banana

Utensils You'll Need:

8 skewers

What You Do:

Thread about four or five pieces of your favorite fruits on each skewer. If you're not going to eat them right away, keep the skewers covered with plastic wrap and refrigerate till you're ready to serve 'em.

My Own Dinner Recipes

Chapter Seven:

Divine Desserts

Nothing beats the sweet stuff, whether you like chocolate or fruity flavors. And once you and your friends learn how to make tasty treats like Rocky Road Brownies or Tie-dyed Jell-O Cake, you'll have more fun than ever! Some of the ideas in this chapter sound pretty wacky, but they look cool and taste great. And they all make great sleep-over midnight snacks.

Apple Crisp

This dessert is perfect to make with a friend—while one of you prepares the filling, the other makes the topping.

Ingredients You'll Need:

Filling

1 tablespoon butter, at room temperature
5 Granny Smith apples, peeled
½ teaspoon cinnamon
¼ teaspoon nutmeg

Topping

½ cup all-purpose flour
¼ cup instant oatmeal
3 tablespoons brown sugar
½ teaspoon cinnamon
3 tablespoons butter or margarine
    cut into pieces, and at room
    temperature

Utensils You'll Need:

Vegetable peeler
Knife
Measuring cups and spoons
2 mixing bowls
9-inch pie pan

What You Do:

Preheat the oven to 350° F. Butter the pie pan. For the filling, peel the apples, cut them into chunks, and throw away the core. Mix the apples, and ½ teaspoon each of cinnamon and nutmeg together in a bowl. Pour the apples and spices into the buttered pie pan. In another bowl, squeeze the topping ingredients together with your clean fingers, mushing the butter into the flour, oatmeal, brown sugar, and cinnamon until the mixture is crumbly and there are no big lumps of butter left. Sprinkle the topping over the apples and bake for about 40 minutes or until you can easily poke a fork through the apples.

Chocolate-Peanut Butter Fudge

The fudgey duo of chocolate and peanut butter creates a cool, layered effect.

Ingredients You'll Need:

1½ cups (8 ounces) chocolate chips
1½ cups (8 ounces) peanut butter chips
1 can sweetened condensed milk
2 teaspoons vanilla extract

4 tablespoons butter
Non-stick cooking spray

Utensils You'll Need:

Small saucepan
8-inch square cake pan
Measuring cups and spoons

What You Do:

Lightly coat your pan with non-stick cooking spray. Over very low heat, stir the chocolate chips, half the can of sweetened condensed milk, and 1 teaspoon vanilla extract in the saucepan until the chips have melted. Remove from the heat and stir in 2 tablespoons of butter, making sure the butter dissolves completely. Pour this chocolate fudge mixture into the square pan and chill in the fridge for about a half hour. Next, melt the peanut butter chips with the remaining condensed milk and vanilla extract. When the peanut butter chips have melted, stir in the rest of the butter, making sure the butter melts completely. Pour the peanut butter fudge on top of the chocolate fudge and refrigerate for about an hour before eating.

Cake Cones

(makes 24)

Decorate these cones with frosting and they almost look like the real (ice cream) thing. Only you know they're filled with a different type of treat!

Ingredients You'll Need:

24 flat-bottom ice-cream cones
1 package brownie mix
  Note: You may need eggs, water, and cooking oil for the brownie mix. Please read the box well and make sure you have all the ingredients you need before you begin.
Frosting (see recipe, page 70)

Utensils You'll Need:

Measuring cups
Mixing bowl
Muffin tin
Aluminum foil

What You Do:

Preheat the oven to 350° F. Wrap the bottom of the ice-cream cones in aluminum foil and place them in the muffin tins (the aluminum foil helps them stand up straight). Make the brownie mix according to the directions on the box. Fill the cones about halfway up with brownie mix. (Don't fill them to the top or the mix will flow over the sides of the cone.) Bake in the oven for 25 minutes or until the brownie is firm. Let it cool completely (about half an hour), and then top with frosting and serve.

Frosting

You can buy prepared frosting or make your own.

Ingredients You'll Need:

8 tablespoons (1 stick) butter, at room temperature
3¾ cups confectioners' sugar
3 tablespoons milk
2 teaspoons vanilla

Utensils You'll Need:

Electric or hand mixer (or a whisk and lots of energy)
Large mixing bowl
Measuring cups and spoons

What You Do:

Beat all the ingredients together in the mixing bowl. If the icing is too dry, add another tablespoon of milk; if it's too wet, add another tablespoon of confectioners' sugar.

Peanut Butter Cream Pie

This creamy pie is a lot easier to make than you think, especially if you start with a prepared graham cracker crust.

Ingredients You'll Need:

1 nine-inch baked graham cracker crust (store-bought
 or see recipe, page 72)
8 ounces cream cheese, at room temperature
½ cup smooth peanut butter
¾ cup confectioners' sugar
2 tablespoons milk
½ cup Cool Whip whipped topping

Utensils You'll Need:

Electric or hand mixer
Mixing bowl
Measuring cups and spoons

What You Do:

Beat the cream cheese with the confectioners' sugar till creamy. Add the peanut butter and milk and continue beating till smooth. Gently stir half the Cool Whip into the peanut butter mixture and spoon into the pie crust; put the remaining Cool Whip back into the refrigerator for now. Refrigerate the pie for at least two hours or until it's set. If you want, you can put a dollop of the remaining Cool Whip on each slice of pie before serving.

Graham Cracker Crust

You can buy a prepared graham cracker crust or make your own. Most of the time homemade food is better, but this is one case where the store-bought kind tastes pretty much like the homemade ones.

Ingredients You'll Need:

Non-stick cooking spray
1 stick butter or margarine, melted
¼ cup sugar
1⅓ cups graham cracker crumbs

Utensils You'll Need:

9-inch pie pan
Small saucepan
Mixing bowl
Measuring cups

What You Do:

Preheat the oven to 350° F. Lightly cover the pie pan with non-stick cooking spray. Over low heat, melt the butter in the saucepan. In the mixing bowl, combine the sugar and graham cracker crumbs and stir in the melted butter till the mixture is sticky. Press into the pie pan and bake for eight minutes or until the crust is crisp. Cool before serving.

Rocky Road Brownies

Have a friend mix the Rocky Road topping while you bake the brownies—as long as you trust her not to eat all your chocolate chips!

Ingredients You'll Need:

1 package brownie mix
  Note: You may need eggs, water, and cooking
  oil for the brownie mix. Please read the box well
  and make sure you have all the ingredients
  you need before you begin.
1 cup chocolate chips
1 cup pecans or walnuts,
  chopped
1 cup mini-marshmallows

Utensils You'll Need:

2 mixing bowls
Measuring cups
8-inch square cake pan

What You Do:

Make the brownies according to the instructions on the box and bake. Stir the chocolate chips, marshmallows, and nuts together in a bowl and set aside. When the brownies come out of the oven, sprinkle them with the chocolate chip, marshmallow, and nut mixture. If you've got the willpower, wait until the brownies are cool to serve them.

Fruit Pizza

This fruit pizza is a yummy dessert that's just as fun to eat as traditional pizza!

Ingredients You'll Need:

Non-stick cooking spray
½ package (9 ounces) sugar cookie dough
4 ounces spreadable cream cheese
½ cup confectioners' sugar
½ teaspoon vanilla extract
2 cups strawberries, blueberries, kiwis, pears, peaches, or any other fruit you like (fresh or from a can)

Utensils You'll Need:

Large baking sheet
Mixing bowl
Measuring cups and spoons
Pizza cutter

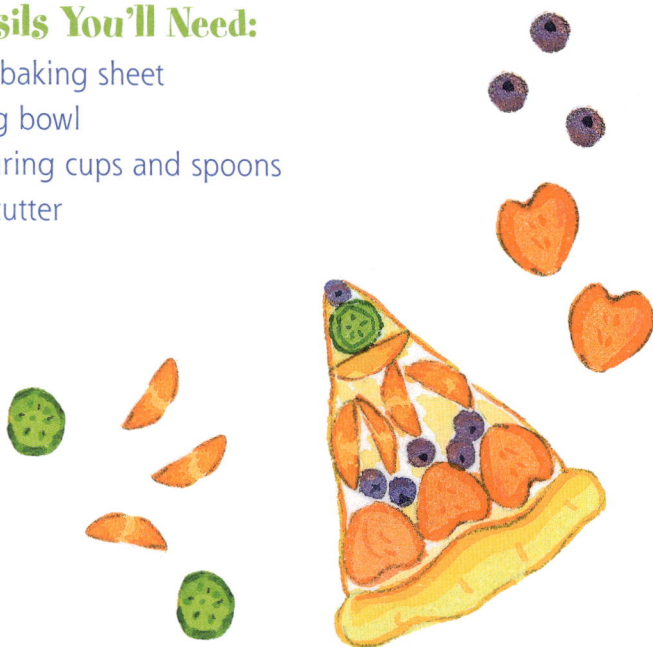

What You Do:

Preheat the oven to 350° F. Spray a baking sheet with non-stick cooking spray. Flatten the cookie dough into a pizza shape. Place on the baking sheet and pop in the oven for 12 to 15 minutes or until the cookie is golden brown. Let cool completely. Mix the cream cheese, sugar, and vanilla extract together until they're well blended. Spread the cream cheese mixture on the cooled cookie crust. Top with your favorite fruit and refrigerate for 15 to 20 minutes before serving.

Tie-dyed Jell-O Cake

From the outside, this looks like a normal cake, but it reveals its true colors when you cut a slice!

Ingredients You'll Need:

1 package white cake mix
   Note: You may need eggs, water, and cooking oil for the cake mix. Please read the box well and make sure you have all the ingredients you need before you begin.
2 3-ounce boxes different Jell-O flavors
2 cups boiling water
1 container of frosting, any flavor you'd like

Utensils You'll Need:

3 mixing bowls
Measuring cups
2 eight-inch round cake pans
Kettle or saucepan
  (for boiling water)
Fork

What You Do:

Make the cake according to the directions on the box and bake in the cake pans. Meanwhile, bring the water to a boil. Separate the two packages of Jell-O into different bowls. Add one cup of boiling water to each bowl, stir, and let cool at room temperature. (Don't add cold water to the Jell-O because you want it to be super-concentrated.) When the cake layers are done baking, take them out of the oven and let them cool completely (about a half hour). When they have completely cooled, poke the top of each layer with a fork so there are lots of little holes. Carefully pour the Jell-O into the little holes. You can make each layer its own color or mix the colors for a truly psychedelic look. Refrigerate for a couple of hours before sandwiching the layers together with frosting.

Crispy Candy Treats

What's a cookbook without some version of a sweet, crispy rice treat? One great way to make them is to use M&Ms, but don't stop there. If you've got the creative bug, try adding a half cup of peanut butter to the melted marshmallows, or cover your crispy treats in melted chocolate. The possibilities are endless!

Ingredients You'll Need:

Non-stick cooking spray
½ cup M&M's candies
3 tablespoons butter or margarine
1 package (10 ounces) marshmallows
6 cups puffed rice cereal

Utensils You'll Need:

Large saucepan
Large spoon
13 x 9 x 2-inch baking pan

What You Do:

Lightly coat the baking pan with non-stick cooking spray. Sprinkle the M&M's evenly over the bottom of the pan. Melt the butter or margarine in a large saucepan over low heat. Add the marshmallows and stir till they melt. Remove from heat. Stir in the rice cereal till the mixture is totally combined. Scoop the mixture into the baking pan and chill till solid. When you cut the treats, flip 'em over so the M&M's are facing up.

My Own Dessert Recipes

....

....

....

....

....

....

....

....

....

....

....

....

....

....

....

....

....

....

....

....

Chapter Eight:
Holiday Goodies

Want to make any occasion super-special? Offer to make something for the celebration: a birthday cake for your best friend's party, Christmas cookies for a holiday party, or a Fourth of July fireworks fruit salad.

Gingerbread People

(makes about 12 cookies)

These gingerbread cookies are great to make during the holidays with friends, since you can each decorate your cookies uniquely.

Ingredients You'll Need:

1½ cups flour
½ teaspoon baking soda
1 teaspoon cinnamon
½ teaspoon nutmeg
1½ teaspoons ground ginger
2 teaspoons brown sugar
4 tablespoons butter or margarine
3 tablespoons corn syrup
   or molasses
Icing (see recipe, next page)

Utensils You'll Need:

Large mixing bowl
Measuring cups and spoons
Rolling pin
Baking sheet
People-shaped cookie cutter

What You Do:

Preheat the oven to 375° F. Mix the first five dry ingredients in the mixing bowl. Melt the butter and corn syrup or molasses over low heat. Stir together the melted butter and syrup with the dry ingredients until they form a sticky ball. Dust a little flour over your work space to avoid having the dough stick to the surface. Using a rolling pin, roll out the dough to about ¼ inch thick. Using the cookie cutter, cut out your cookie people, place them on the baking sheet, and bake for about ten minutes. Decorate cookies with icing.

ICING

To add some extra flavor and fun to your gingerbread people, you can buy prepared icing or make your own.

Ingredients You'll Need:

½ cup confectioners' sugar
1 to 2 teaspoons water
Food coloring

Utensils You'll Need:

Spoon
Plastic baggie or pastry bag

What You Do:

Mix the water with the confectioners' sugar. To make different colored icings, add a little food coloring powder or gelatin to the mix. Place in a pastry bag or plastic baggie with one of the corners cut off to pipe on decorations.

Sweetheart Sugar Cookies

(makes about 25 cookies)

You'll need a heart-shaped cookie cutter to make these Valentine's Day treats to give to your friends. (If you don't have a cookie cutter, you can cut out heart-shaped dough with a knife.)

Ingredients You'll Need:

1½ cups flour
¼ teaspoon salt
¼ teaspoon baking powder
1 stick of butter at room temperature
¾ cup light brown sugar
1 egg
½ teaspoon vanilla extract
1 tablespoon milk

Utensils You'll Need:

2 mixing bowls
Measuring cups and spoons
Electric or hand mixer
Plastic wrap or a sealable
  baggie
Rolling pin
Baking sheet

What You Do:

Preheat the oven to 350° F. In a mixing bowl, stir together the flour, salt, and baking powder. In the other bowl, beat the butter slowly, adding the brown sugar until the mixture is light and fluffy. Beat in the egg, vanilla extract, and milk until well blended. Beat the dry ingredients into the butter mixture in two batches until your cookie dough is smooth. Scoop up your dough and wrap it in plastic wrap or a sealable baggie. Refrigerate the dough for at least an hour. After the dough has chilled, dust a little flour over your work space to keep the dough from sticking to the surface. Using the rolling pin, roll out the dough to about ¼ inch thick. Cut out your hearts, place them on the baking sheet, and bake for about ten minutes or until golden brown. Decorate the cookies with red sprinkles, colored sugar, or icing (see recipe, page 83).

Green Slime

Perfect for Halloween, this green Jell-O and Gummi worm creation looks gross but actually tastes pretty good. You can make this recipe in a glass bowl, or you can place your worms in an ice cube tray and fill it up with Jell-O for bite-sized pieces of creepy fun!

Ingredients You'll Need:

1 package lime Jell-O
1½ cups boiling water
1 cup cold water
1 cup ice cubes
10 Gummi worms

Utensils You'll Need:

1-pint (2-cup) glass bowl
  or an ice cube tray
Mixing bowl
Measuring cup

What You Do:

Make the Jell-O according to the speed-set directions on the box. Pour half the Jell-O into your glass bowl or ice cube tray and refrigerate for a half hour or till it's solid. Leave the other half of the Jell-O on the counter at room temperature. Sprinkle your Gummi worms on the refrigerated portion of Jell-O, then pour the remaining Jell-O over them. Refrigerate the whole thing till it's solid.

Birthday Cake Supreme

This is the most chocolaty, gooey, delicious cake ever, and best of all, it's a lot of fun to make!

Ingredients You'll Need:

1 package chocolate cake mix
   Note: You may need eggs, water, and cooking oil for the cake mix. Please read the box well and make sure you have all the ingredients you need before you begin.
1 fourteen-ounce can sweetened condensed milk
1 twelve-ounce bottle caramel sauce
1 seven-ounce can whipped cream
3 crushed toffee bars, like Skor or Heath

Utensils You'll Need:

Measuring cup
2 mixing bowls
13 x 9 x 2-inch baking pan
Wooden spoon

What You Do:

In one of the bowls, mix the cake according to the directions on the box and bake in the pan. In the other mixing bowl, combine the condensed milk and caramel sauce, and stir until well blended. When the cake comes out of the oven, poke a bunch of holes in it with the handle of the wooden spoon. Pour the condensed milk and caramel sauce mixture into the holes, then let the cake cool. When the cake is completely cooled, cover it with the whipped cream and sprinkle it with the crushed toffee bars. Yummy!

Fourth of July Fruit Salad

Wow your friends and family this summer with a red, white, and blue fruit salad—a patriotic dessert for a perfect Fourth of July picnic.

Ingredients You'll Need:
2 cups blueberries
2 cups strawberries
2 bananas, cut in coin-shaped slices
½ cup orange juice
1 tablespoon sugar

Utensils You'll Need:
Measuring cup and spoons
Cutting knife
Serving bowl

What You Do:
Wash the blueberries and strawberries, then cut the bananas into coin-shaped slices. Put all of the fruit in your serving bowl, add the orange juice and sugar, and mix well. Then serve!

My Own Holiday Recipes

Conclusion

Hopefully you've found some recipes in this book that you can't wait to try out with your buds! Don't worry about having too many cooks in the kitchen—there's no such thing! As you'll find with most of these recipes, there's always something someone can do, whether it's chopping, stirring, keeping an eye on the oven, or cleaning up. And once you start cooking, you'll realize it's really not as hard as it might seem— especially when you have lots of help! You and your friends might even be inspired to experiment a little and come up with some recipes of your own. It's hard to think of another hobby that's so much fun *and* produces such tasty results when you're all done!